Mystery Pose

A Yoga Guessing Game

Published in the United States by Savasana Press

Rockville, MD

ISBN 978-1-7367283-0-7
Library of Congress Control Number: 2021905240

For permissions or other information, please visit the author's website at:
www.shiningkidsyoga.com

Cover and interior design: Amy Morrison

Background images by canva.com

Disclaimer: Always listen to your body when doing the yoga poses included in this book. If anything hurts or feels uncomfortable to you in any way, please stop immediately. If you have any health conditions or injuries, please consult with a doctor prior to practicing yoga.

To learn the correct pronunciation of the Sanskrit words in this book, visit:
www.shiningkidsyoga.com/blog/mysteryposesanskrit

It's time to play a guessing game

To unravel the clues
and uncover each name

See how many poses
you can guess and do

Remember, I believe in you!

Root down as you grow tall

Grow your branches,
watch the leaves fall

Stand on one foot,
Bend one knee

Reach up high I am a...

Tree

Vrksasana

Wrap one arm under,
Cross one leg over

I spread my wings and soar
over hill and clover

On my perch I look so regal

Up in a tree I am an...

Eagle

Garudasana

Reach one arm up

Kick your other foot
back and grab it

Find a spot to focus on as you start

Lean forward and open your heart

Think hard before you answer
I move with grace, I am a...

Dancer

Natarajasana

On top of the water
standing tall

I'm number 2, there are 3 in all

One knee bent and legs out wide

"Surf's up, dude!" I say with pride

I can be called many names,
I will answer to either-or,

I'm a ... or ...

Surfer or Warrior

Virabhadrasana II

Arms stretched out, body in a T

All the birds like to follow me

I balance on one foot
as I soar through the air

From place to place I travel
without a care

I'm not a rocket ship,
but I'm described by my name

Up in the sky, I'm an...

Airplane

Virabhadrasana III

I look like an upside down V

The most famous yoga pose
is known as me!

Hips up high, hands and feet down low

I'm all bark no bite, don'tcha know!

With cats and kittens
I refuse to dialogue

I'm wagging my tail because I'm a...

Down Dog

Adho Mukha Svanasana

I am a shape, I have three sides

Stretch your arms out
step your feet out wide

Lean over with one arm up and
one arm down

Keep your head parallel to the ground

Keep focused, don't let your body tangle

I'm not a square or circle, I'm a...

Triangle

Trikonasana

High in the sky, I glow bright at night

I go through several phases
which are in plain sight

I'm not full or crescent,
I'm not even waxing

People gaze at me and find me relaxing

Though we're in the same galaxy,
I'm still far away from Neptune,

Look up! I'm a....

Half Moon

Ardha Chandrasana

Squat down, separate your feet

Stick out your tongue and catch a
fly to make this pose complete

Animals like me live in a bog,

At home on my lily pad, I am a...

Frog

Malasana

Across the sea we row and row

Waves rocking us to and fro

Life is but a dream,
we know this song, every note

We're on the clear blue sea
setting sail in a...

Boat

Navasana

Lying in the grass I slide and slither

Skin leathery, sparkling like glitter

Don't be afraid,
don't tremble and quake

I just like to "hiss"
because I'm a...

Snake

Bhujangasana

Knees apart, feet together

My antennae are up,
I'm light as a feather

Flying in the air, looking like royalty

Wings of many colors,
flapping for all to see

I'm the prettiest of all the insects that fly,

Emerging from my chrysalis, I am a...

Butterfly

Baddha Konasana

I blossom in the spring,
I smell very sweet

You can get into my pose by
bringing your arms under your
calves and hands next
to your feet

As you balance and blossom take a
deep breath in and feel your power

Pink, yellow, and blue,
I'm a beautiful...

Flower

Vitasitakamalasana

On top of a present I proudly sit

I lie on my belly, bend my knees, and
reach for my ankles for just a bit

I wait with all the other gifts
sitting in a row

Wrapped up so pretty, I am a...

Bow

Dhanurasana

In the desert I proudly roam

I kneel up high,
arch my back,
and put my hands on my tailbone

I am known for my hump,
I'm a very unique mammal

I can go for weeks without water,
I am a...

Camel

Ustrasana

Forehead on the ground,
curled up like a ball

When you need a break,
on this pose you should call

Take deep breaths as you
rest and repose

Close your eyes, we're relaxing in...

Child's Pose

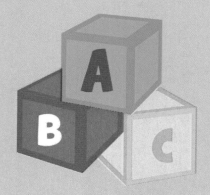

Balasana

I rest in my crib,
lying on my back

I bend my knees and reach for my
toes as I rock in my sleep sack

I'm not crying, definitely, not maybe

My mom is so happy 'cause I'm a....

Happy Baby

Ananda Balasana

Yay, you've done it,
you've discovered them all

You kept your balance, you stood tall

You stretched your mind and body
as you uncovered each pose

To meet the challenge
you bravely rose

Now it's time to rest,
lie down on your back

Close your eyes,
arms by your side, and relax

Breathe in peace,
breathe out bliss

Have you ever felt a
moment as calm as this?

Remember this wisdom:

You shine bright like a star

You are whole, perfect,
and complete exactly as you are

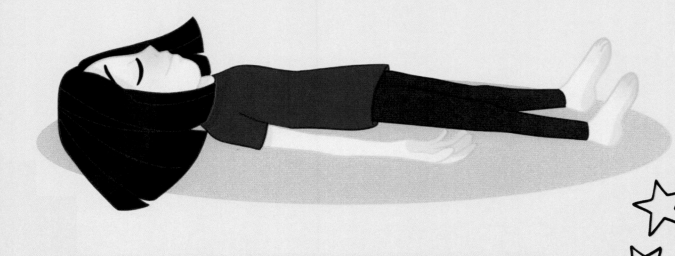

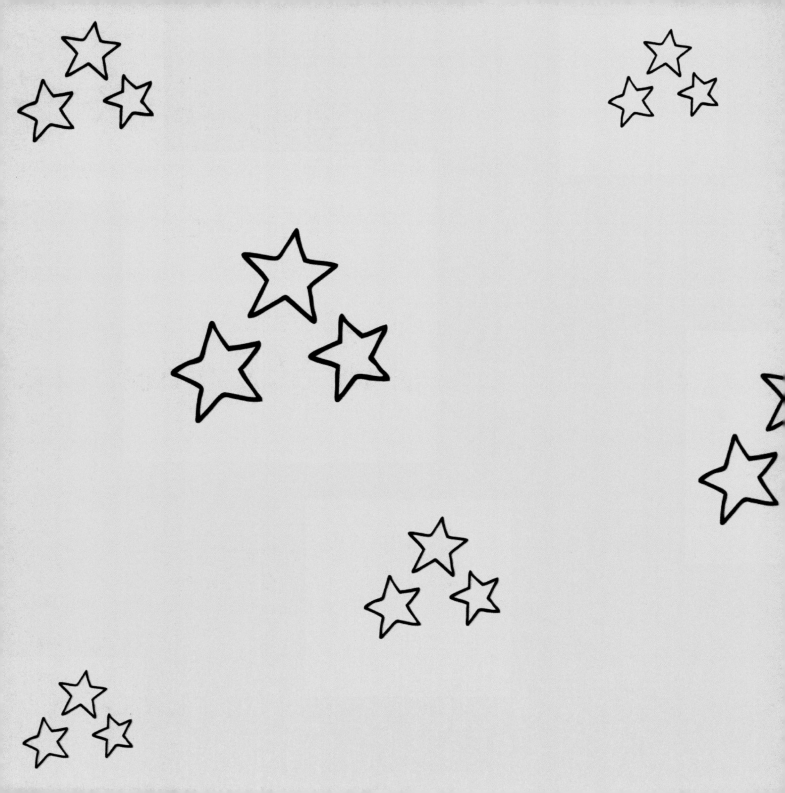

Andrea Creel, Author

Andrea is a registered yoga teacher and the founder of Shining Kids Yoga. She loves creating games, songs, and stories to make yoga fun and accessible to children.

Andrea lives in Maryland in a home filled with pink walls, purple sofas, a cuddly cat, and the world's best son.

To contact Andrea, visit her website:
www.shiningkidsyoga.com

Deran Deegala, Illustrator

Deran Deegala is an aspiring young digital artist who loves doing freestyle drawings and drawing original creations. He is an honor roll student at his middle school and enjoys empathizing with people.

Besides art, he enjoys playing video games, reading, and spending time with family and friends. Deran lives with his family in Rockville, Maryland.

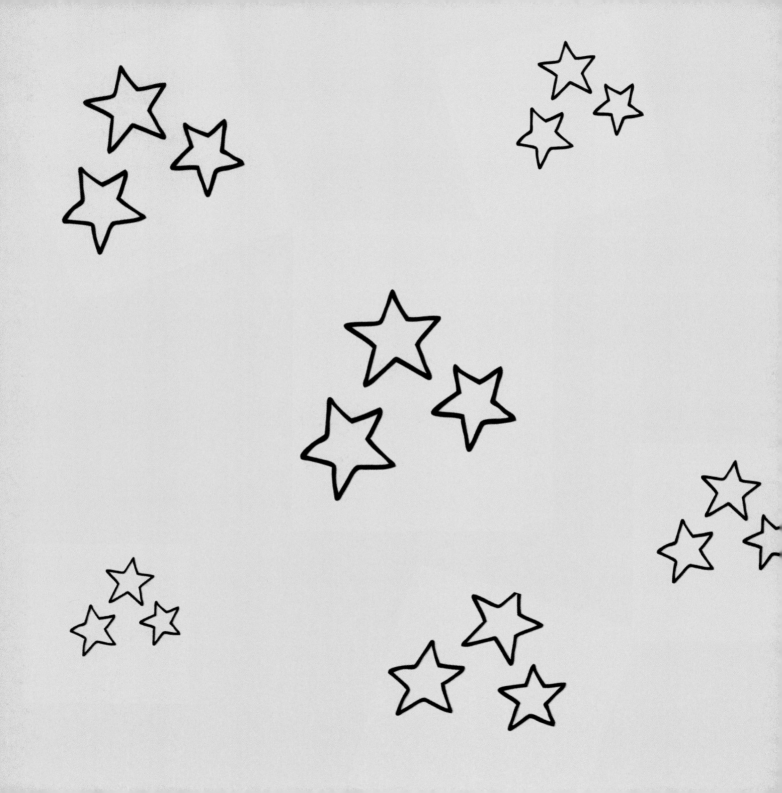

Made in the USA
Middletown, DE
26 April 2021